Self Confidence

(Tips and Tricks on How to Gain Self Confidence)

(By Robert Gallagher)

Table of Contents

Preface	2
Introduction	5
Importance of Self-Confidence in our Daily Lives	9
Factors That Impact the Early Development of Self-Confidence	24
Tips & Tricks on How to Gain Self-Confidence	34
Other Books Written by Robert Gallagher	68
References	69

SUBSCRIBE TO MY NEWSLETTER

http://eepurl.com/U76qr

Preface

Have you ever found yourself in the situation where you really wanted to take on a new challenge but just had to rule it out because you lacked the self-confidence? Are you stuck in a tedious nine-to-five job, having found the ideal job for you elsewhere but just don't dare to apply for fear of rejection? Did you want to join that gym but not have the confidence to turn up wearing shorts? Did you wish you had the faith in yourself to pass that exam, or ask that pretty girl out you fancy? Are you trying to summon up the courage to walk across the beach in a new swimsuit? Or failing to make friends at school or college for fear of ridicule? If you have just answered yes to any of these questions, then rest assured that this book has specifically been written for you!

I am Robert Gallagher, and for you, I am a friend who is going to stand right by you and make it possible for you to deal with all of these problems. I will help you realize that these are common place issues that people go through every single day of their lives. The reason why I wrote this book is because I am the sort of individual who has a willingness to listen to others' problems and make it possible for them to find solutions. In the past, I have suffered from a lack of self-confidence but have overcome this and would now like to share the secrets I have gained with you to give you the opportunity to succeed in life, to meet those challenges, which once you would have had to decline, overcome your insecurities and consequently enable you to lead a happier and more fulfilling life.

The basic purpose of this book is to help you deal with the problems that you are facing and help to resolve them. Before doing so, you need to be aware that these solutions are only possible if you are mentally strong. I hold the belief that our problems are often triggered by events which have taken place in our past; events which are hard to shake off and overcome. These issues can be so strong that they can actually end up slowly poisoning us on a daily basis. The target of this book is **YOU** – Every single person out there who is suffering from symptoms of a lack of self-confidence. My target is every man and woman and child out there who suffers from this inhibiting negative perception of themselves.

I can assure you that by going through this book, you are going to gain self-confidence, the amazing power which will enable you to deal with situations of adversity on your own, and come out as a real winner in this world that is nothing short of being prejudiced and unfair. The past two years of my life have been spent on carrying out considerable research and on studying the works of those who specialize in being able to provide you with all the right knowledge so you can have a better and happier future. I should like to thank everyone who stood by me in this respect and especially those who supported me in the process of writing this book - your book.

SUBSCRIBE TO MY NEWSLETTER

http://eepurl.com/U76qr

Introduction

Self-confidence is the realistic perception of one's own judgment, ability, and power. To have a true belief in yourself is important because it gives you the capability of doing even the most mundane of everyday things. Without a certain degree of self-confidence, we would all be prevented from going to work, meeting our friends, going out in public or, at its worst, even leaving the house. Self-confidence is deemed to be a positive trait as we feel that we can make a valid contribution to conversations, offer our perspective without fear of ridicule, and feel that we have every right to be a crucial member of the community. These are all prerequisites to leading a normal, healthy, and enjoyable life. Without this belief in ourselves, we would dwell on negative thoughts of failure, insecurity, and possibly even start to develop phobias and irrational fears. Having a low opinion of ourselves can be seen as an error in our perception, an incorrect way in which we process information.

Admittedly, we all lose our self-confidence at times – this is quite normal. The loss may arise due to a number of different factors, but how we deal with these feelings and recover from this detrimental state of mind is most important. In this book, the author endeavors to identify some of the reasons why we might suffer from a temporary loss of self-confidence and gives the reader some useful insight and recommendations for alleviating these negative thoughts and succeeding in regaining one's self-confidence again, possibly even to greater heights than before.

The terms self-confidence and self-esteem are used interchangeably nowadays, but the notion of these positive perceptions of oneself dates back to the late 1800s when eminent psychologists, such as John Dewey and William James, proposed that these traits were crucial to the achievement and success of a human being. The term self-esteem refers to how you feel about yourself overall and develops from specific experiences or situations. Self-confidence, however, refers to how you feel about your abilities and can vary depending on each situation.

Many theories have been proposed since that time, although, it is generally agreed that possessing self-confidence is a salient characteristic of a person's happiness.

Self-confidence holds immense importance in our lives. It is what gives us the power to perform to the best of our abilities on a day to day basis – it is what gives us the fuel to meet new challenges continually thrown at us throughout life. Truth be told, if you lack self-confidence, you are going to continually doubt yourself, have second thoughts about your talents, skills, and abilities, and basically question every initiative that you want to take in life. Those who lack self-esteem or self-confidence often turn out ironically to be the sort of individuals who start hampering their very own progress in life. This is because they are never interested in trying out new things, bowing to their irrational fears and unrealistic perceptions. In cases where the lack of self-confidence reaches unprecedented heights, it prevents the sufferer from making any attempts in life to attain success. The reason for this lack of interest in attaining success is rather simple: the person holds no interest whatsoever in reaching new heights of success for the simple reason that they fear failure because of not having any faith in their very own abilities. The major problem with this is that they continue to struggle with feelings of inferiority to all those around them. The worst part is that a majority of people who suffer from confidence related issues know deep inside that they hold a lot of potential and yet they simply refuse to acknowledge it. For this very same reason they pass through life with an extreme fear of failure.

If we allow them to become established, we can reinforce the feelings of guilt, inferiority, and unworthiness; these emotions are learned and not a fixed part of our personality. If we keep on believing them, we will never break through the negativity. The Law of Cause and Effect supports this view. Our thoughts are the causes and conditions are the effects. Therefore, if you continue to believe these negative thoughts, they will become the reality. You must do everything in your power to re-learn more positive thoughts of yourself, your achievements, capabilities, and qualities. This, in turn, will give you greater self-confidence and get you on the track to succeeding in life.

People who lack self-confidence simply don't have what it takes to succeed in life. The reason is simple: they have no faith in their own abilities, have no control whatsoever over their lives and are referred to as 'push-over's' – they let those around them rule their life. They are inhibited by the restrictions placed on them by themselves. Conversely, people who are self-confident are positive about their abilities, never question their skills, and accept themselves for who they are – unaffected by others' opinions and criticism, they are in command of their own lives. It is for this very reason that it is highly recommended for people who lack self-confidence to pay attention to a couple of tips and tricks available to them to be able to take a more positive approach towards their lives and start developing more trust in themselves – they need to develop their self-confidence to be able to succeed in life and, most importantly, to enjoy all that life has to offer!

Importance of Self-Confidence in our Daily Lives

"The moment you doubt whether you can fly, you cease forever to be able to do it" –J.M. Barrie

In the quote above, J.M. Barrie quite admirably sums up the importance of self-confidence in our daily lives. When we doubt our capabilities, we place limitations on ourselves as to whether we can achieve something or not. These limitations endure, and we start to believe we can never do anything about them. We should, instead, take the stance of Theodore Roosevelt, who told us to,

"Believe you can, and you're halfway there"

In order to achieve a particular goal in life, it is necessary for us to possess certain amounts of discipline, skills, capability, determination, and most of all, self-confidence. This particular bit of self-confidence comes from the possession of the right types of skills, as well as clarity in terms of the goals that need to be achieved. A mind and body that is capable does not provide an individual with what it takes to function to the best of their ability until the time that these are backed up by self-confidence. If truth be told, our self-confidence is the pivot over which everything creative as well as analytical capability of the human brain relies upon. It is for this reason that it is believed that a lack of self-confidence has the potential to greatly impair the workings of not just the mind but the body as well, which in turn leads to some disastrous failures.

In life, it is just not possible for us to achieve great things if we do not have the desired level of confidence. If you lack in self-confidence, even the best of skills and capabilities are not going to get you anywhere. This is because low self-confidence has the potential to prevent you from moving forward in life, thereby making it impossible for you to take any initiative at all. It's as if it actually paralyzes your mind and body when the time to take certain decisions comes up. You need to remember that this life works wonders for those who are confident, for confidence has the potential to make or break your life like nothing else can. You need self-confidence if you really want to bring out the fighter hidden within you!

You need to bear in mind the basic fact that our self-confidence or self-esteem as some may refer to it, has the potential to influence every single aspect of our lives. It is that very factor that determines how much we get to achieve in our lives. The thing with self-confidence is that it affects you emotionally, mentally and in certain cases, physically as well. It is actually an attitude that makes it possible for people to have positive and even realistic views of not just their lives but every situation that they encounter as well. However, being self-confident in no way means that the individual has what it takes to achieve everything in life – it merely provides them with the potential to put in the best of their efforts into everything that they do, without having to question their ability and even give a single second thought about it at all.

The sad thing about people who suffer from a lack of self-confidence is that they are extremely dependent on the approval given to them by others in life, in terms of what they should do, how they should act, and sometimes even what they should wear. They have no control whatsoever over their lives, and simply don't think it is possible that they can ever be successful in life. Even if they receive a compliment, they are prone to ignoring or even discounting it for the simple reason that they think they don't deserve it. Instead, they tend to counteract the compliment with some self-deprecating comment, which in turn makes others less likely to offer nice comments in the future owing to the bad reaction. On the other hand, those who are self-confident actually go against what others have to say, for they have complete faith over their own abilities – they know and like who they are and don't think that it is necessary for them to conform to the likes of others just to be accepted in society.

Self-confidence and how it can impact your professional life

The presence of self-confidence in one's personality has the potential to help people achieve greater levels of success. It is this which drives them towards the achievement of their goals and objectives in not only life in general but in their professional life as well. Although it is possible even for people that lack self-confidence to achieve quite a lot in life, the only difference is that they simply don't have what it takes to enjoy their success and accomplishments. To them, nothing is ever enough, which in the long run makes them end up being pure workaholics. On the whole, it can be claimed that self-esteem is just what drives one towards success and allows them to enjoy the successes too!

The fact of the matter is that if you wish to achieve something in life, it is necessary for you to take risks for it. As we all know, there cannot be a gain in life without pain. However, have you ever considered what it is which gives a person the inclination to get up and take a step forward, while there is another who is continually being held back? SELF-CONFIDENCE! Yes, it is just the confidence that we have that allows us to come out of ourselves, and take on leadership roles even if we end up meeting with failure in the long run. Achievers and failures are basically differentiated by this one point – the level of faith that we have in ourselves.

There are countless men and women in history who have succeeded for the simple reason that they possessed great quantities of self-confidence. It is because of this particular element that they took initiative in their lives and broke down the shackles imposed on them by a secure and highly paid job, just so they could fulfill their dreams of being able to set up their very own business. Of course, the only thing that gave these seemingly ordinary people the potential to break through their nine-to-five routine in order to instead become successful and affluent entrepreneurs was solely the faith that they had in their dreams and in their own personalities for the most part.

In order to receive recognition, be noticed, and be visible around your workplace, it is necessary for you to portray yourself as a naturally self-confident person. Anyone who wishes to acquire success in their careers needs to be confident. There's no other alternative. Don't believe me? Well, take a good look around your organization – what do you notice? It is evident that the successful ones have personalities which are brimming with self-confidence and they totally know how to show it off. However, the one thing that you need to remember is that you must never let your self-confidence reach a level where it becomes egocentric or unbearable to others (Nov, 2013). This is known as 'over-confidence' and is certainly not deemed a desirable trait.

The fact of the matter is that every single organization these days tends to have its very own culture. For this reason, it is necessary for your confidence levels to be reflective of the ways in which other employees at your workplace practice their confidence. Moreover, the sort of dynamic world that you operate in these days is going to throw endlessly changing situations and countless conflicts at you. It is in situations such as these where your self-confidence is going to be particularly necessary and help you through. It isn't going to be easy, let me tell you that beforehand. However, with your confidence, it would be possible for you to maintain your composure and deal with whatever situation has come up and in the most professional manner possible.

Another thing that you need to know about self-confidence within the workplace is that it makes it possible for you to focus and work on things that are normally way beyond your comfort zone. Getting used to a particular routine and becoming comfortable with specific work habits is extremely easy. However, if you have the right degree of confidence, it would be easily possible for you to push things forward and even work outside of your comfort zone. The best part is that you would be able to achieve all of this with the utmost poise. Whenever a change comes about within your organization, you would find that all of the other employees would be following you by example for the simple reason that they would desire direction from someone who seems to know what they are doing, who has a positive attitude towards their approach and practices it in a very confident manner.

Confident individuals are the most successful of individuals – this is one fact that no one in the world can deny. Whilst in the work place, such individuals have the potential to become role models who are followed by all other employees. With your self-confidence, it would be possible for you to soon make it possible and relatively easy for others to adapt to changing circumstances and situations. So, if you really want to stand out amongst the rest at your workplace, make sure that you take your self-confidence to work with you and take things to the next level! You will very shortly reap the benefits, get noticed by your employers and begin to be offered promotion, new and interesting tasks and ultimately be earning a higher salary.

Today's world is extremely competition based. In this world, self-confidence isn't merely an asset. It lays the foundation which creates the basis for your overall survival. Note that when it comes to your professional life, securing a particular job is dependent upon being invited to an interview and once in that interview room you have to demonstrate that you possess the necessary skills to make you capable of carrying out the tasks which you will be set. Whether you feel the confidence to assert yourself in this way is never easy in the interview situation but what is important is that you at least seem confident. Gaining the confidence will inevitably come when you receive that phone call to say that you've actually got the job. Later, when it comes to attaining a salary increase, you again need to be confident at work to prove yourself worthy of it. Unfortunately, only the ones who are confident are the ones that get recognition at work. The attention that they receive is just what brings to them admiration and acceptance and it is this acceptance that brings peace and surplus amounts of energy to them, which consequently plays a major role in their overall efficiency. It is this efficiency that is generated through your confidence that helps you become an achiever, and in the long run, the achievements that come your way have the knock-on effect of adding to your self-confidence.

Possessing self-confidence is like possessing a magical spiral. How come, you ask? Well, because when you gain utmost levels of confidence in yourself, riches and happiness do not linger too far behind you. For this reason, it is necessary for you to have utmost belief in yourself – just tell yourself that you have all the potential in the world in yourself and things will just be fine. Because at the end of the day, those who think that they can win are actually the ones who end up doing so!

Self-esteem and our relationships

> "Becoming self-confident allows you to be assertive, ask for what you want and set limits on what you don't want. That includes asking for a commitment if that's what you're after!" – Dr. Shirley McNeal

People who are emotionally healthy and exude self-confidence typically have the potential to have long-lasting relationships. We need to acknowledge that people who have low self-confidence or low self-esteem just do not have what it takes to appreciate themselves – to them, they just aren't the perfect fit. They suffer from an emotional void that can only be filled by acquiring others' approval. They indulge in indecisiveness, negative thoughts, and are extremely judgmental towards their own selves, which has a major impact on their relationships.

On the other hand, people who hold utmost confidence in themselves are the ones who are endowed with the ability to love, respect, and give time, importance, and attention to not just themselves, but those around them as well. Self-confidence plays a major role in determining just how deep and potent our relationships are going to be.

Wonder how, at times, the bald guy gets to swipe those beautiful ladies off their feet, while the handsome one just stands there staring at them? Of course – it's because the bald guy oozes self-confidence, whereas the handsome hunk does not! It's the self-confidence that makes the ladies fall head over heels for the bald guy!

The fact of the matter is that low self-esteeme doesn't have any considerations at all for sex, race, age, marital status, religion, weight, height, or any other factor at all. The worst part is that there is no way at all that you can prepare yourself to face the wrath of low self-confidence. However, there is a good chance that you can change it – it just takes a bit of patience, practice and a small amount of hard work to turn things around for the better.

The thing with people with a lack of self-confidence is that they have particular traits associated with themselves. For starters, they are continually found indulging in what has been labeled as being 'negative self-talk'. This includes things like, 'I am just not worthy of having a loving partner', or, 'There's no reason why any lady out there would want to date me', or, 'There's nothing special about me. Why would anyone want to date me?" Another aspect associated with these people is that they are overly critical, which gets to a point where they start acting extremely destructively towards themselves. They are always found doubting themselves, and continually apologize to those around them for any mistakes that they think they might have made. The worst part about them is that they just don't have what it takes to receive, accept or even acknowledge compliments, and continually require feedback from others. Another truly devastating aspect associated with them is that they become so much of a perfectionist that it becomes impossible for them to even achieve and fulfill the most basic tasks, for the simple reason that they have a severe fear of failure.

Now, in terms of relationships, you need to show self-confidence as it is evident in everything that you do. Ever noticed how a bad stain right in the center of a white T-shirt doesn't ever get missed? Well, the same holds true for self-confidence – no one ever fails to notice it. It is one of the most off-putting characteristics in a person, which is the reason why in the long run it proves to be truly detrimental to their relationships. What this means is, that if you suffer from a lack of self-confidence, there is no way that you would be able to get into a long term or steady relationship. Your partner would need to spend all of their time offering reassurance and trying to boost your confidence. This is an unrealistic demand to expect of them and in the end they will get fed up of doing this. So, if you are trying to form a relationship with someone, be it a boyfriend, girlfriend or just form a new acquaintance, while having this low self-confidence and such a low opinion of yourself, you may be fighting a losing battle and have the opposite effect on them, which would make them less inclined to want to get to know you in the first place.

The worst part about low self-confidence is that it makes you so vulnerable that you end up trying to find love and commitment in all the wrong places, with the wrong person and for all the wrong reasons. Think of it this way, have you ever dedicated yourself wholly and solely to one single person in the hopes that they would reciprocate your love and affection, only to find that you were being taken for granted? If you suffer from a lack of self-confidence, there is a good chance that you have already suffered from such a scenario and, ironically, may have brought about the situation yourself.

When it comes to relationships, a lack of self-confidence turns a person into a type of toy which can be manipulated by those inclined to take advantage of this weakness. They convince themselves that they aren't really worthy of being loved, whereas on the other hand, they expect the other person involved in the relationship to prove otherwise and love them to the core. Such a state of affairs is not just damaging and demoralizing but rather self-defeating as well.

The one fact about we humans is that we just end up assuming that people are seeing us in a manner that is similar to the one in which we perceive ourselves. For instance, if we think that we are friendly, warm, and funny, then we would assume that people also think about us in a similar manner. Hence, those who have immense self-confidence and perceive themselves as being positive individuals, assume that people will perceive them the same way. To them, there is a good chance that people who haven't met them yet are still going to find them interesting and automatically like them and that they will be loved and adored by everyone around them.

On the other hand, those who suffer from a lack of self-confidence aren't really positive about the ways in which people perceive them. They continually have doubts about the ways in which people would perceive them, for which reason they refrain from socializing. Most importantly, they forever have doubts as to whether the people they know now will continue to like them, or feel they would end up hating them with the passage of time due to their failures. A very important thing for you to know about people with low self-esteem is that it isn't necessary for them to be continually negative about their personalities. At times their problem is more of an episodic nature, and they suffer from what is known as 'fluctuating self-esteem'. In such cases, their self-confidence changes according to the events of the day, on their mood etc. Most importantly, they have masses of self-confidence in certain aspects of their life, whereas others are marked with a severe lack thereof. For instance, they might think that they are extraordinary at work but consider themselves a major failure in their personal relationships.

The reason learning all of this is important for you is because being humans, we have an inborn tendency to react towards people in the same way that we think they perceive us. If we believe that a particular person likes us or holds us in high regard, we will be more positive towards them. However, if we have made up our minds that a particular person doesn't like us, or isn't too comfortable in our company, then we are more likely to hold an intensely negative approach towards them. Now, considering that people who have a lack of self-confidence just don't have the sort of mindset that allows them to believe that they are being unconditionally loved, they continually hold themselves back from giving their utmost to a relationship. They end up being vulnerable and engage in the sort of behavior that, in the long run, repels their partners away and drives them away.

However, at times, being in a relationship actually has the tendency to increase an individual's self-esteem. For instance, let us consider that your partner thinks that you are a wonderful person who is extremely talented and very attractive then, over a period of time, you are surely going to come to appreciate yourself more and more. You are going to start believing in the views that your partner holds of you. Despite this, the one hurdle that you would need to overcome is that of actually beginning to acknowledge that your partner holds you in extremely high regard and loves you for the person you are.

Factors That Impact the Initial Development of Self-Confidence

Many psychologists contend that our personalities are formed in our early years and are as a result of the way we are brought up. Sigmund Freud (1856-1939), best remembered for his theories of personality development believed that we pass through several stages of development, from birth through to adolescence, when our personality becomes fully developed. He proposed that a child will focus on the various erogenous zones of the body until he reaches adolescence but if he gets fixated on any of these zones, or stuck at any of the stages of development, this will consequently affect his personality as an adult, when it is too late to change and improve.

A more feasible (and perhaps more believable) explanation was put forward by Erik Erickson (1902-1994), who proposed his Theory of Psychosocial Development. Once again believing that personality is developed in stages, he said that if, between birth and one year old, a child feels mistrust towards its caregiver, it will feel anxious and become paranoid. Between the ages of one and three, the child begins to assert his autonomy. He will show signs of wanting to explore his environment and requires the freedom to do this unhindered by others. If, therefore, the child's caregiver or parent restricts his movement, prevents him from exploring, or is constantly over-critical of his actions, the child will become dependent on others and begin to demonstrate a lack of self-confidence. From this, we can see that our parents may have had quite a substantial effect on our self-confidence as adults, and it is very important to acknowledge this now. That despite these theories, there **is** a lot we can do to change our personalities and, in particular, increase our own self- confidence and strategies to help us will be covered in some depth in Chapter 3.

Our self-confidence can be threatened in our early years if we have a younger brother or sister who is highly capable. Furthermore, if you have a sibling who is close to you in age, people are more likely to compare the two of you as you grow up and if others perceive your sibling as more capable, this will act as a reinforcer of your low self-confidence. This can cause jealousy, friction and disharmony within the family, all impacting on your opinions of yourself and ultimately on your later achievements. Social psychologists have likened this reaction to a fuel gauge. Leary (1999) asserted that this 'gauge' warns us about threats to relationships which might cause social rejection. This, in turn, motivates us to act more sensitively towards others' expectations of us. Social rejection lowers our self-confidence but strengthens our desire to seek approval. Being outcast by others makes us feel inadequate, unloved, and unattractive. On the plus side, this warning light can motivate us to take action to try and improve ourselves and seek acceptance and more fulfilling relationships elsewhere.

Research shows that we tend to believe that we have an inherent tendency to strive towards our full potential. We all begin life with a natural curiosity, creativity, and the need for discovery. If we are left unencumbered by the restrictions which society places on us, we will develop and become fully functioning human beings. However, sometimes, society imposes conditions on our worth as people do not accept all of our opinions, behavior, or attitudes. It is when we are inhibited from reaching our potential by society and significant people in our lives, that we develop low self-confidence and begin to perceive ourselves as inept, unworthy and unlikeable. Any successes we have then are perceived as due to luck or as an omen to future failure. With low self-confidence, we tend to exaggerate our limitations and minimize our accomplishments. Basically, it is a vicious circle, one which makes a person expect failure and indulge in self-criticism.

People who suffer from low self-esteem have often experienced significant disapproval from their parents. Bad parenting styles entail failures being punished and successes either being ignored or unrealistically high expectations being imposed on the child. For example, by consistently telling him that he ought to be achieving higher grades at school, a child, who is confusingly praised by his teachers on the one hand but criticized by his parents on the other, is inevitably torn between the two opposing factions. This lack of control over his destiny, produces feelings of helplessness, low self-confidence, and he could possibly give up trying as hard as he believes his parents would be disappointed in him in whatever he does.

You can easily see from these scenarios how an individual can be affected from childhood through to their adult life by the thoughtless acts of others. The worst thing is, even if we do not agree with the way in which we were brought up ourselves, we very often find ourselves speaking to our own children in the same way. Admittedly, it is a hard cycle to break and one which is particularly evident in the European culture.

In opposition to these theories of child development and early experiences as being the basis for us having self-confidence as adults, Biological psychology argues that having a low opinion of ourselves can be seen as an error in our perception; an incorrect way in which we process information. Our biological composition suggests that there is a particular part of the brain which is often responsible for these faulty perceptions. This key structure in the brain, the amygdala, can elicit fear and foreboding in us if our neural circuitry is not functioning properly. This can inevitably impact on our self-confidence and prevent us from taking on new challenges, being in the slightest daring or risking any new experiences. This all sounds rather worrying but wired up incorrectly or not, we can learn to dull these heightened emotions and compose ourselves to deal with day to day challenges and, thereby, increase our self-confidence. Some tips to facilitate this will also be covered later on.

There are many different factors that have the tendency to impact the early development of self-confidence in one's life. The attitudes that parents hold typically tend to have a major effect over the ways in which children perceive themselves right from the beginning of their early childhood. Parents for this reason need to be very accepting of their children and their personalities for this way, children are then more likely to feel good about themselves in general. On the other hand, if the child's parent, or, worse still, both parents, take on a critical role, become demanding, or even take up an obsessively overprotective approach and thereby limit the independence that children enjoy, this situation would set the cornerstone for the child to start thinking that they aren't capable of much at all, or that there is something wrong with them.

In order to develop a child's self-confidence, it is necessary for parents to be more encouraging towards their child's progression towards self-dependability, be more accepting of the inevitable mistakes that the child makes, and show their child unconditional positive regard. Abraham Maslow's 'Hierarchy of Needs' argued that we would never reach 'self-actualization', the highest and most desirable point of our lives, unless we received recognition and respect by the ones who mean most to us without conditions being imposed on them or by others trying to make us into people we just were not. This is particularly important in helping children to start learning how to appreciate themselves and to be more confident about their own personalities. There are many more things a human needs besides food, water, oxygen, and a safe place to sleep. This unconditional positive regard, particularly provided by one's own parents or caregiver in our early years, helps us to attain our biggest goals in life, experience true happiness, and basically function well in every respect. To enable us to be a 'self-actualized' person, we must be able to perceive reality accurately, focus on our problems rather than on ourselves, to be self-sufficient, independent, and identify with others, allowing us to create a bond with them. We do not need a whole lot of friends to be able to do this, perhaps just a few really good ones who take us at face value and do not try to either change us or condemn us for the things we say and do.

One of the most important stages of our life for the development of self-confidence is adolescence. This is a time when a young adult is very self-conscious of their appearance and what others think of them. During this period, they begin to make the transition towards caring more what their peers and friends think than basing everything on the opinions of their parents. They show the ability to perceive themselves from the perspectives of others at this stage of their lives. Having a positive perception of their body image for example correlates highly with their self-esteem. Similarly, social acceptance of their peers can play an important role in increasing their confidence. Many adolescents believe that in order to be popular you need to be physically attractive and this is one of the reasons why the body image is so salient at this stage. At the opposite ends of the scale, those who think little of themselves and have low self-confidence are those more likely to suffer from a lack of social skills, depression, anxiety and ultimately achieve less academically in school. Girls are particularly vulnerable to the effects of having low levels of self-confidence during puberty. It is quite frequent that girls have a distorted image of their own bodies and how they appear to others during this time. The support of an important role model in their lives, and not necessarily one within the family environment, is extremely important for all adolescents, both boys and girls, especially if there is any chance of them being bullied and taken advantage of as a result of their low self-confidence. If an adolescent believes that their parents show an interest in them, they are much more likely to be self-confident. Many studies have found that a consistently high level of self-confidence prevents a child from giving in to inappropriate peer pressure, misusing alcohol, or taking part in other deviant behavior. This may include taking drugs, getting involved in crime and teenage pregnancies. These findings are particularly valid for any adult who works with children at this point in their lives as, how the adolescent is handled, can impact on them later on and affect their interpersonal relationships.

The thing with self-confidence is that its lack isn't typically associated with a lack of ability. If truth be told, it is typically the outcome of having focused excessively on unrealistic demands that are set upon us by others, particularly by our parents initially and the society at large. Even the way that our friends perceive us, or treat us tends to have a major impact over our self-confidence. It is for this reason that students who are in their college years typically have the tendency to re-examine their personalities and this is where the influence of their friends begins to have the utmost importance. Instead of the competition shown between younger school children, always vying for the attention of others, their parents, teachers and other peers, in higher levels of education it can be quite readily seen the support (both moral and educational) which your fellow mates can provide you. These are friendships which can endure through our lifetime and are based on trust, companionship and on the fact they were there for you when otherwise you might have given up and let the lack of self-confidence get the better of you.

To this end, we can see that many factors may influence the initial development of our self-confidence and how the involvement of significant others in our lives can make so much difference at every stage. Low levels of self-confidence may have been imposed on us through poor parenting skills or mistrust of our caregiver. In turn this might make us a maladjusted individual who is nervous of every situation and of forming new friendships. Those who are less self-confident are more likely to give in to peer pressure, participate in delinquent behaviour and possibly to perform badly at school. Later on in life, our relationships with others are affected and we don't have the motivation to push ourselves towards success. On the other hand, those of us with higher levels of self-confidence have usually been allowed the freedom to explore as small children and have been shown the utmost support up to and throughout our adolescent years For this reason, the more self-confident individuals have often been well-adjusted individuals who are more popular, they have been enabled to meet new challenges head on, have succeeded in their academic achievement, experienced more fulfilling relationships, enjoyed better mental health and are able to cope with stressful situations.

Tips & Tricks on How to Gain Self-Confidence

As noted in the previous chapter, there are many different ways in which we can gain and improve our self-confidence. Some of these factors are covered in this section. Here's a look into a few of them that are sure to help you out:

- **Assess what you want most in life**
Sadly, we are all on this planet for a relatively short time, so it is essential that we get the most out of our lives and are able to get the satisfaction out of the things we most enjoy. For this, it is a good idea to sit down and consider the things you want most. By this I don't mean possessions but:
What do you want to do which would make you most proud?
What do you most want accomplish in the next year?
Base your assessment on what would make you the most happy, or what would give you the biggest sense of achievement or make you the most excited. Identify what you are best at, and try and formulate a plan to combine your abilities with your goals. Nothing is unachievable – you just need to keep focused on the things you want most.

- **Work on your strengths and emphasize on them**

No matter what it is that you try or achieve, make sure that you give yourself credit for it. What basically happens is that when you start focusing on the things that you can do, you actually appreciate yourself for the efforts that you have put in, instead of worrying about the end results that you have or should have achieved. We all have the ability to accomplish something, you just need to identify what it is that you want to achieve most, and practice the skills that will enable you to succeed in it. The most important thing is that you have belief in yourself.

- **Don't accept failure**

The old adage, 'if at first you don't succeed, try, try, again', is appropriate to consider here. Don't give up after you are not able to do something the first time. There is no such word as can't, what you mean is that you don't think yourself capable of achieving it, and therefore, inhibit your own abilities. Instead, keep trying until you can actually do it. Don't consider yourself a victim of failure – this is not true. With determination, practice, and persistence, you will achieve the things you most want out of life. Passing a driving test, for example, is not out of the realms of possibility. All you need to do is get out there on the road, have a few more lessons, ask your instructor how you can improve your driving techniques and keep on practicing all those components which you find hardest. It doesn't come down to whether we feel we have lots of self-confidence or not. This will come naturally when you succeed in the things which matter most to you. Don't give in after the first adversity you encounter. Gaining self-confidence will come with practice, repetition, and a self-regard for your abilities.

- **Start taking small risks in life**

Instead of considering new experiences in life as occasions where you get to win or lose, you need to see them as opportunities where you would get to learn something and maybe achieve something from participating. This way it will allow you to open yourself up to new possibilities, thereby making it possible for you to appreciate yourself, your strengths and personality more. If you don't ever try to take small risks, you will become stagnant and end up impeding your own growth as you will take every single opportunity as a means of encountering outright failure. Perhaps dare to take a small risk every day. You will soon find how much fun is involved, and even though it may make you a little nervous at the time, you will notice that sometimes, you will get what you want out of the challenge. Think of it more as having an adventure.

- **Don't worry about others' opinions of you**

Self-confident people tend to interpret feedback the way they want, but if you are less confident, you might be very concerned about how others see you and think about you. We might believe that other people see us in a bad light, but this is not often the case. Maybe you have misinterpreted that 'funny' look you were given or read the way a person spoke to you in the wrong way. It is actually highly probable they don't hold any opinions of you at all, and if they do, they are very unlikely to all be negative ones. If it bothers you that much what they think, confront them, and ask for an honest opinion. You can then be honest in return, and come to a mutual decision that you hope to deal with the reasons they dislike or mistrust you. You will try to make them see that you are much nicer than they first thought but, in return, you will expect them to act in a different way to you as well. Basically, start again with them, and the best way to achieve this is by having mutual respect. They will undoubtedly have more respect for you for doing this.

- **Self-encouragement**

Any detrimental assumptions that you have in life can easily be countered with the help of self-encouragement. This way, all harmful assumptions are easily replaced by ones that are more reasonable, factual and practical. Let us consider an example here. If you run into a situation where you think it is necessary for you to achieve outright perfection, indulge in self-encouragement and tell yourself that although not everything can be done perfectly, you will nevertheless give it your best shot, endeavor to put in the best of your efforts and do the very best you can at it.

This way, you would be in a better position to accept yourself and appreciate the efforts that you are putting in for whatever you wish to achieve, whilst at the same time being realistic about the things that not only you would not be capable of achieving but others too.

- **Carry out a self-evaluation**

You need to learn how to appreciate yourself on an independent basis. This is extremely important because doing so makes it possible for you to avoid the stress that is caused from depending solely on the opinions that others have formulated about you. When you carry out a self-evaluation, you can more readily change the way you behave and how you feel about your personality. You basically get to acquire a strong sense of self, which helps you escape from the overriding control that you hold over your own life and which you perceive others to hold over you as well.

- **Refrain from comparing yourself to others**

It is easy to feel envious of another man's girlfriend, his brand new sports car, his well-paid job, or his holidays in exotic locations, but maybe he damn well deserves them! You too can have these things (well maybe not his girlfriend) if you get up off your backside and start having faith in yourself. I'm sure his extravagant life style is not all it's cracked up to be - his car costs a fortune on the insurance and still breaks down on occasion. He probably chooses to go to Hawaii when there's a hurricane storm brewing, and let's face it, his girlfriend's expensive clothing will be substantially eating into his budget. She probably has bad breath too! The grass is not always greener on the other side, so be happy with you've got, be grateful for small mercies, and break the habit of believing that you are inadequate. Maybe it's the other guy who is and not you.

- **Overcome your insecurities**

Replace all those self-deprecating comments about yourself with positive ones. If it helps, start listing them, and then, relay them during the course of conversations to other people too. For example, if someone should ask you if they can discuss a problem they are experiencing with you, tell them that not only the problem will be discussed in complete confidence but that you are also a good listener. Make sure you reassure them that their secret will be safe with you, and let them appreciate how honest and kind you are. You have lots of positive qualities, so make sure others know about them too. If you always find it uncomfortable and embarrassing to walk into a public bar on your own owing to your perceived lack of confidence, don't go into denial of this and decide never to go into a bar alone again. Overcome this insecurity by doing it more often. After a couple of times, you will find that it has no effect on you. You will actually enjoy going into a bar and meeting your friends.

- **Be prepared to accept a compliment**

    If we constantly negate a comment which is intended to please us and refuse to accept a compliment, a vicious circle begins, whereby, we believe that we are right. For example, if someone says, "I like your shirt", make sure to say a simple, "Thank you". That is all which is necessary. If you start being self-deprecating and say things like, "oh, it's only a cheap one", or "it's just a hand me down from my brother", people will stop complimenting you, and you will have reinforced your own negative views of yourself by counteracting the nice gestures of the other person. Instead, feel proud of yourself for having been complimented in the first place, tell others what the person said, and start believing that you have possessions, traits, and skills worth having after all.

- **Compliment yourself**

    Congratulate yourself for all the little things you achieve during the day. We all do something worthwhile during the course of a day, whether it is selling something to a customer at work, changing a flat tyre on our bike, making someone happy with a cup of tea or finally getting round to sending off that payment for the refuse collection bill. It is easy to overlook the good things we do every day and dwell on the bad things which happen instead. These things are often out of our hands anyway, so there is no point blaming ourselves. If it helps you remember what you have achieved at the end of a week, keep a diary. You will be surprised by what you have tackled, and now, you can give yourself a pat on the back to acknowledge those amazing qualities you have and what achievements you have made.

- **Refer to some motivational quotations to give you a new perspective**

"Don't wait until everything is just right. It will never be perfect. There will always be challenges, obstacles and less than perfect conditions. So what! Get started now. With each step you take, you will grow stronger and stronger, more and more skilled, more and more self-confident and more and more successful." ~Mark Victor Hansen

"Low self-confidence isn't a life sentence. Self-confidence can be learned, practiced, and mastered — just like any other skill. Once you master it, everything in your life will change for the better." ~Barrie Davenport

"If you hear a voice within you say 'you cannot paint,' then by all means paint, and that voice will be silenced." ~Vincent Van Gogh

"Confidence comes not from always being right but from not fearing to be wrong." ~Peter T. Mcintyre

"If we all did the things we are capable of doing, we would literally astound ourselves."
"Talk to yourself like you would to someone you love."
~Brene Brown

"Embracing your true self radiates a natural beauty that cannot be diluted or ignored. Confident, powerful, untamable, badass you!" ~Steve Maraboli

"True beauty is the flame of self-confidence that shines from the inside out." ~Barrie Davenport

"Trust yourself. You know more than you think you do."
~Dr. Benjamin Spock

- **Find other positive output**

    From time to time, it is a good idea to refer to other material which can show us how to gain self-confidence. There is a plethora of information out there designed to help us in that respect. Look for an appropriate video clip on YouTube, for example, or look at a motivational blog or two on Twitter. Better still, start writing your own. It is especially helpful if you log in every day or so to add your own inspirational material. It not only gives you the opportunity to sit back and contemplate what you are capable of, but it also helps to increase the self-confidence of others. There are books at the library and electronic books on the Internet which can all offer ideas for motivating you and helping to increase your self-confidence.

- **Join a group**

By joining a group, whether it be the local football team, knitting group, hockey team, Mother and Baby group, chess enthusiasts or bell-ringing for beginners, you will experience a sense of togetherness which strengthens our self-concept and boosts self-confidence. The strong respect we develop for our group also gives us pride in ourselves. It prevents you from continually thinking about your individual successes and failures and places emphasis on your successes and interests as a team. You have people to whom you can relate, and this will give you a different perspective on reality and increase your belief in yourself.

- **Make a list of your past accomplishments**

At first, you might think you have achieved little in life, particularly if you are at a low ebb and not too proud of yourself at the moment, but certain things have made you feel this way, and it will all change if you put in a little effort. Start back as far as you can remember. Perhaps you were the best at spelling in your class when you were, say, eight years old, or received a basic gymnastics award. Later on, you might have joined the school orchestra or choir and played in a concert to a lot of parents and children. Did you give your parents a pleasant surprise when you passed your mathematics exam or did well at English? You should be able to think of quite a few things now, and they don't all have to be academic. You don't always have to be really clever to achieve things in life. Look at Bill Gates, for example, who got nowhere at school and is rumoured to have got expelled. He is now massively rich and famous, he just decided he was going to do well in his own business and succeeded. If you currently have employment, you should list this, as many people don't have a job. You got chosen because of certain skills, qualifications or abilities – what are they? What did you tell that employer which enabled you, rather than someone else, to get the job? Have you recently fixed a leak, decorated a room or saved up and bought a new piece of technology? Write it down. It is an achievement. You made it happen, and you should be pleased with yourself. Bask in your achievements, hang up that certificate you got for passing a course, put that photo on the hall table of you receiving that sports trophy or of your graduation as constant reminders that you were, and still are, a worthwhile citizen who has much more in life to offer.

- **Boost your own morale**

    Make a list of your own qualities. At first, you will find this a hard task to do, but when you have thought about it for a few minutes, you will be surprised how many positive attributes you can enter on the list. This is a well-established technique used in counseling and also in classes aimed at promoting leadership and management skills. The technique also has the useful effect of boosting your confidence not only at the time of constructing the list but also later on when you can refer to it when, for whatever reason, you are feeling a little less confident again, perhaps before an interview or special date and just need to be reminded how worthy you are. You don't need to go to the lengths of Mohammed Ali when he kept reciting his famous confidence boosting chant, "I am the greatest!" but instead, use your own self-affirmations to re-affirm that you are in control of your thoughts, actions and emotions.

You may even get the list out again, from time to time, to add new qualities which you have identified. Who knows, you may even put some of them on your curriculum vitae or in a job proposal when otherwise you were lost for words and suffering from a writer's block. Suitable suggestions of adjectives to get you started may be: honest, kind, hard-working, conscientious, friendly, sincere, passionate, caring, humble, and calm. After a week, look at the list again, and see if you could add more, confident-sounding qualities to the previously listed ones. For example: determined, persistent, positive and courageous. Once you acknowledge you have these traits, you will always possess them No one can take them away from you.

- **Choose your friends well**

    It is a good idea to have a good mix of friends. If you feel like you suffer from low self-esteem or are low in self-confidence, try to spend time amongst people who you know are more confident. You may think this would make you feel worse, possibly even make you feel like you are more inferior, but this is not the case. You will admire them for not worrying what others think of them – they are just being themselves, and people accept them that way. Their mannerisms, the confident way in which they hold forth in a conversation, and the way they can walk with their head held high, are all indications of a healthy self-confidence and are traits which will rub off on you too. Of course, if people over over-confident and seem big-headed, people may not see this as desirable and, if you watch for the reactions of those around that particular person, you will see they are ridiculing them behind their back and do not really want to be associated with them. It's all about reaching the best level of confidence –not too much and not too little. Basically, by just being natural and not always putting yourself down when you're with others, is a nice happy medium. Likewise, try and spend time with supportive people. There is no point associating with so-called friends who mock and ridicule you or boast about how well they are doing all the while, how much they are earning or which nice car they are buying next. You must be able to respect yourself, and this cannot be done whilst others are reveling in taking away that confidence again.

- **Learn a skill or trade**

No one is suggesting you suddenly take up rocket science here, or that you sign up to a course on the dynamics of molecular physics in order to boost your self-confidence but perhaps by finding something which interests you, maybe at a local school or college, this will help you to see yourself in a more positive light. You could go and pick up a prospectus of the courses available and have fun choosing from the long list of possibilities. A friend of mine, for example, suffered from a terrible loss of self-confidence from the effects of a violent and abusive partner. She made the right decision to leave the unhappy marriage but was left with feelings of failure and inadequacy. So, she signed up for a basic course at the local school, and after a few weeks, found that not only did she enjoy the course and the social life it offered her, but she was also quite good at it. This inevitably increased her self-confidence and made her work at it even more. In fact, along with the positive support she got from her fellow class mates and the tutor as well, she went on to take the subject at a more advanced level and finally ended up getting a high level degree and a subsequently well-paying job that went along with it. Perhaps we can't all be that successful, but what we can do is find something which takes us out of ourselves and introduces a new interest in our lives, be it a pottery course (we all love the film 'Ghost'), flower arranging, calligraphy, or perhaps a basic plumbing course or car do it yourself sessions. Whatever your choice, it only takes up one or two evenings a week, but it gives you something to be proud of and something different to talk to other people about, rather than just going to work every day and lounging about on the sofa all evening when you get home. It will do wonders for your self-confidence. You see!

- **Have a good exercise regime**

It has long been noted that regular exercise has a beneficial effect on our state of mind as well as our body. Exercise focuses the mind and brain and helps to control our emotions. It can also help change a particular mindset which we might be harbouring inside. Chemicals known as endorphins are released in our brain which make us feel happier and more energetic. They act as nature's own pain killers too. Exercise gives us the feel good factor and helps us to restore our minds to a state of composure after (and before) stressful situations in our lives. If we sit at a desk all day or behind the wheel of a car, pent up stress, anger and resentment all accumulate making our heart beat faster and allowing anxieties to fester without release. This is particularly bad for our state of mind as at some point these manifested problems will become too onerous, and we will 'explode'. We might, for example, be abrupt to someone in the workplace who gives us too much work, hoot aggressively at other road users, or show other forms of road rage, use expletives even though normally we might hate to do so, and generally take out our frustrations on those we care for at home. Exercise is an excellent cathartic release, and after twenty minutes on a cross-trainer, exercise bike or treadmill, we can take on the world again with a fresh vigor, a different perspective, and a more willing freshness. Tai Chi and yoga classes are good for overall suppleness and for relieving us of pent up anxieties. We do not, however, need to join an expensive gym to get the exercise we need, but just do a few minutes of gardening or housework. Anything at all which gets us moving is good for us. Walking is also a great way to allow us to free ourselves of all those negative thoughts we have when things are getting on top of us. Just being out in the fresh air works wonders for relieving us of the cobwebs and generally making us feel healthier and more focused. Perhaps you live near a public baths and can go once or twice a week to swim a few lengths. You'll soon notice how much better you feel. Your body will be much firmer, your stomach much flatter, and you'll be less inclined to smoke or drink alcohol for fear of ruining your newly found healthier you. Once again, we can feel proud of ourselves for looking after our body as well as our minds. We will feel much more confident and reduce the chances of stress-related diseases, heart attacks and stroke. After a short amount of time, you will also notice how taking part in a little exercise each day gives you more energy, to tackle the rest of your day.

- **Set yourself achievable goals**

There are several ways in which you can achieve this, and thereby, improve your self-confidence. After you have exercised a few times, set yourself little goals. These goals must be SMART goals, the acronym for Sensible, Measurable, Achievable, Realistic, and Trackable (or Time-related). Perhaps you go swimming. The first few times, you might only feel capable of swimming a few widths of the pool. Well, the next time you go, try to swim ten widths, then fifteen, then twenty, and so on. After a few weeks, you might try one or two lengths and gradually increase the amount until you are swimming for the entire time you are in the pool. The same goes for walking. A twenty minute walk is all well and good on a nice day, but you spend half of that walking home again, so you don't get very far. Take a drink with you, and walk twenty minutes both ways. Next week, walk for a whole hour and sit somewhere to admire the view, read a book, or enjoy a coffee before you make the walk home. Download an application on your phone and monitor your progress. It is great to see how far you have cycled, how many steps you have walked or, how many miles you have run. Such an app can also tell you how long you have spent on a particular activity and how many calories you have expended. You will soon reap the benefits of the small targets you set yourself as you will feel good about yourself and clear your head ready for the next challenges to be faced.

- **Reward yourself**

This is most important while you are putting in all these efforts. By this, I don't mean reward yourself for all that hard work in the swimming pool with a big fat cream doughnut, but treat yourself to a body treatment, a massage, or pedicure etc. Just spend some 'you time' chilling out in a quiet stress-free environment. If you have been particularly exerting yourself and doing lots of exercise or gardening, make sure you reward yourself with a nice cup of tea and perhaps watch that DVD you've meant to get round to watching for some time. As the TV advertisement for that well-known chocolate bar suggests – 'Work, Rest, and Play'. Ensure you have enough of each.

- **Improve your employment prospects**

You do not need necessarily to be unemployed to carry out these simple techniques, although it has long been identified that unemployment does account for a lack of self-confidence and self-esteem in a lot of people (Winefield, 1997). Being without a job can inevitably make an individual feel like he has little to offer the world, he may develop as sense of having no future and nurture feelings of inferiority and alienation without having a reason to get up every morning. The longer time goes on, the self-fulfilling prophecy will kick in and his belief that he won't get a job will actually prevent him from getting one. There are however ways of dealing with this Catch 22 Situation. First, the person must formulate a curriculum vitae, bringing all their details up to date, their contact details, qualifications, courses attended etc. Get someone else to check this through and see if they can help add a few more personal attributes that the person hasn't thought of themselves. Make it look professional, not flowery, and be sure to omit fancy fonts, colors, and different styles. Sign up to receive emails of available jobs in your area, buy the local newspaper, look in shop windows for advertisements for labor needed, and better still, go into any places for which you would consider working and ask to speak to someone in their Personnel Department. Most cities have an employment office which has advisers you can talk to who can help you find something suitable for you and tailor it to the hours you would prefer and to match your skill set. Finally, these establishments often hold mini courses, workshops and discussions on employment related issues such as how to do well at interviews, writing a good cover letter or how to sell yourself in a job application form. That is what they are there for and gaining some form of employment gives you a reason to continue and will do wonders for your self-confidence.

- **Do something constructive**

    One of the contributory factors towards feeling you have low self-confidence is purely boredom (Frydenberg, 1993). There is always something you can do to prevent yourself from being bored. I am sure you can make your own list but here are just a few ideas to get you motivated: pick up a recipe book and choose something to make which makes your taste buds water. If you don't have the necessary ingredients, get out there and go and buy them. Choose a book to read and read the first few chapters. If you don't have an old favorite on the book shelves at home, go to the local library or book shop. Go on the Internet and make a wish list of all the things you would buy if you could afford them. Put them in order of priority, and buy one for yourself when you next get paid or feel like you have accomplished something you are particularly proud of. Phone a friend or arrange to go and see them. It gets you out of the house and gives you something to look forward to, plan it, do it and enjoy the memories afterwards. You want more ideas? No, you need to think of them for yourself. If you're bored, look for something to do. Once again, you'll think more highly of yourself for doing it.

- **Indulge yourself in your favorite pastime**

    Make sure you don't spend all your time buried away in your tedious daily routine of working, eating, and sleeping. Find something you can be passionate about;

something you have always wanted to take up, or something you used to do but, until now, had forgotten about and just kept on putting off, thinking you would get around to it again someday. You could go and play a few holes on the golf course, get out those paint brushes and canvas again or dust off that old camera and take some pictures or re-tune your old guitar and practice a few chords. Every single person alive has some form of talent, and it's up to you to develop and nurture it, enjoy it and then share it with others who will appreciate what you can do. It doesn't need to be anything creative. Not all of us can paint, draw, or play a musical instrument. Perhaps you have an old favorite fountain pen and like to write in beautiful hand-writing. Having a friend or 'pen pal' in another county, state or another country is ideal as they would love to receive a hand written letter from you. Nowadays, people just resort to a hastily tapped out and abbreviated text, an abrupt email, or spontaneous notification on Facebook. To take time to tell someone how you are feeling, what the countryside looks like at this time of year, or what is growing in your garden is much more personal and makes the recipient feel very special. You have personalized the letter because you have written it yourself, and they have grown to know you better because you've used your own words and used your own style of writing, instead of an inaccurate spell checker or predictive text! If you still find it difficult to cultivate your own ideas or feel like you don't possess any talent, approach a volunteer group. They will be extremely grateful for the smallest contribution of your help and time and they will soon find things you can do and show you that there is nothing so rewarding and confidence building as helping those most in need. There are always charitable organizations just waiting for people like you to go along and give them some support. Just check out your local Yellow Pages for details or ask in your nearest library or church for details.

- **Boosting the self-confidence in children**

If the centre of your concerns is not yourself but your child, there are many ways in which you can help them to feel more positively towards themselves. We all notice the sort of parent while we are out and about who constantly reproaches their child for everything they do. "Don't do this", "Don't do that", "Don't touch that, you disgusting little child" "Why do you keep playing with that? It'll make your hands dirty" and so on. The child might be displaying inappropriate behavior, but the poor thing just doesn't know what he can do! This overly critical parent doesn't realize that what is happening is that the bad behavior is getting rewarded by way of receiving attention from the parent(s), which in turns reinforces this type of action from the child. What about handling this a different way, and either making time to have a conversation with the child or distracting him from the things you don't want him to do? Perhaps attract their attention by pointing out another child and commenting on their good behavior, polite manners, or how they play nicely with other children. Then, your child may wish to be more like that other child and copy their actions accordingly.

We must lead by example. It is a well known fact that we are our own children's role models. If we don't want our children to be critical of others, don't sit there yourself and talk about Mrs. Jones as being miles too fat and ugly or comment that Mr. Smith deserved to get the sack from his work for being lazy. Your child will soon take on these traits too and not be very liked for them. Instead, try to restrict your comments to positive ones, both of your child and other people too. Your child will soon believe this is appropriate and continue to do this himself. Some educational authorities have realized that it is important to reward good behavior rather than castigate the bad behavior. If the naughty child sees that he can in fact do something right and get rewarded for it, he will continue to repeat these appropriate behaviors, and this will, in turn, boost his self-esteem and liking for himself. Social learning theorists have indeed found a correlation between self-confidence and academic achievement. The well-adjusted child who doesn't continually receive attention for his inappropriate behavior will believe he is as good as his peers and begin to concentrate in class and consequently succeed more in his education. No one likes a disruptive child at school; it can make life a misery for the teacher, the child, and his class mates. The bottom line is, identify those things your child actually does right and make them feel good about them. Encourage good behavior, but always try to disregard the bad behavior and let it pass by unnoticed.

- **Help others in need**

If we are looking for ways in which to increase our self-confidence and feel good about ourselves, there is no better way than to achieve this by helping out others at the same time. It is not being suggested that you alter your will to leave all your money to that beggar in the street or paint a person's whole house for no recompense whatsoever. It is the little things which count and which people are so grateful for. Hold a door open for that little old lady who is struggling with her bags, press the button on the lift doors so that the parent with the stroller has time to get in, offer to make someone a cup of coffee at work when they are extremely busy, rather than just making your own, and offer to do the clearing up after a meal when your partner is obviously dead beat; these are all things people will thank you for and will make you like yourself more. They might not seem substantial efforts at kindness at the time, but they are just the sort of things for which get you remembered as 'that helpful guy in the Customer Services Department', 'that kind lady at Number 12' or 'that wonderful boyfriend, I have'. It is surprising how you will be rewarded too – pocket money for your children, a cup of tea from a grateful neighbor, a thank you letter sent to your boss, or merely an appreciative smile. All these things will enhance your self-confidence and make you glow with pride.

- **Don't dwell on perceived failures**

Stop thinking of the things that go wrong in your life as failures... they are conversely <u>delayed successes</u>! Unfortunately, our negative thoughts, if we don't fight against them, will impact on our actions and guarantee the undesirable result we should have chosen to avoid. If, for example, we believe we won't pass an exam, we won't study and revise for it. If we don't think we can drive a car, then we might not try in our lessons and never buy that dream car we have always wanted. It is necessary to change our attitude and consider ourselves just as capable as the next man. Someone might ask you how many times it took to pass your driving test. It is so easy to automatically say you have failed three times. Word it differently (if you have to tell them at all), by saying you are nearly ready to take your test. You have not failed, you just haven't passed yet, but you will! If you haven't reached the required grade in an exam, research more, practice harder, repeat, revise and study more. You <u>will</u> pass next time. It'll be on a different day, you'll be using a different pen and be wearing a charm or carrying a mascot to bring you luck but overall it will be you who has ensured you pass with 'flying colors'. More importantly, you will be carrying that new found self-confidence you have earned by putting in all that extra work. Be proud of that and you will benefit from the effort.

- **Congratulate yourself**

    You often see people talking to themselves when they are out and about. Ever wondered what they are saying? Most often they are talking through a scenario and offering themselves encouragement. You will hear runners and cyclists struggling near the top of the hill, mumbling "come on, you can do it", or workers carrying a heavy load, chanting "just twelve more and then I can go home" or a person at a gym doing sit-ups, breathlessly saying "nine hundred and ninety two, nine hundred and ninety three" ... etc. These people are motivating themselves to achieve something that they otherwise would not be able to do, and they won't give up until they have done it. Admittedly, they might look a little weird talking to themselves, but it works! You should do the same (but maybe in private). Have a two-way conversation, and ask yourself just what it is you are frightened about. When you tell yourself that you don't think you can knock on the boss's door and ask him for a salary increase tomorrow, re-assure yourself, and give yourself reasons why you think you deserve it. Pretend you are speaking to your boss or manager, and confidently tell him the things you have done for his business for which you seek recognition. Whilst you are doing this, you are not only giving yourself ideas but practicing the conversation at the same time. This repetition will help you to remember what you were going to say when actually faced with the situation in his room. Talking to yourself in the shower is a private place where you can boost your own confidence without the interference of anyone else (unless you're taking too long in there and family members are hammering on the door!) Praise yourself, say well done for all the good things you have done that day, and wish yourself luck for the challenges coming up. Remember to tell yourself that you are very capable of accomplishing these challenges and can reward yourself with a nice glass of beer or your favorite meal when you have attempted to meet them. You can always do this sub vocally as well, so there is no chance of anyone overhearing you.

- **Give psychological support to others**

Praise people when they do good things, and avoid criticizing them when they do things you don't approve of. If you support others while they are feeling a bit under the weather or suffering from a lack of confidence, they will appreciate this and be more likely to return the favor when you feel this way too. Maybe they are getting over the effects of a failed exam, a driving test, a missed opportunity for promotion, or a temporary loss of confidence as a result of a partner who has jilted them. Whatever the cause, you can offer your sympathy, but don't allow yourself to get dragged down by their feelings of depression and gloom. What is suggested here is that you offer them kind words of encouragement to help them back on the road to recovery, and as soon as you see signs that they are making an effort to see things differently again, praise them, slap them on the back, or merely acknowledge their recuperation with a 'like' for their efforts.

- **Increase your social network**

If you only have one or two friends, you will only have their opinions and points of view to consider. The more friends you have, there will always be someone you can contact for moral support, just like they will have you too. Acquaintances are not quite the same thing as friends, they are merely people you have met once or twice but they can be just as useful to you at times. These people can often help you find a mechanic for your car, suggest a good restaurant if you want to impress someone you're taking out, or help you to write a job application. Join a social network like Facebook, and see how many of your friends and coworkers are on there already. You will soon be surprised how many of them regularly put a notification on, so it's a good way to keep in touch with old friends as well as make new ones. Lost touch with that girl you got on so well with in second grade? Do a search for her on there, and see if you recognize her from a picture even though it might be twenty years ago or so. You will be able to boost your confidence by having an ever escalating number of friends, and even add friends of your friends as you get to like the things they write too. You can set up a reminder of when their birthdays are to wish them well or simply 'poke' them just for fun. Have a look on Twitter too to see what other people are doing. Many people regularly put a 'tweet' on there, so you can keep up-to-date with the latest conversations about football, fashion, or what some naughty TV personality has done. All these things take your mind off yourself and might prompt you to do some of the interesting things others are having a go at.

- **Show off that new found self-confidence**

    Now, you are beginning to feel more confident in yourself, put it to your advantage, and show others that you are experiencing it too. Small acts convey our self-confidence, such as the following:

Dress appropriately for the occasion – if it's a formal occasion, wear a shirt and tie if you're a male and a smart skirt and blouse if you're a female. In an important meeting or interview, you might have heard it referred to as 'power dressing'. It has the benefit of eliciting good first impressions on others which endure over time.

Maintain good posture – sit up straight, don't slouch, and keep your hands still on your lap. Never slouch or yawn as this can be taken as disinterest in what someone is saying to you.

Keep eye contact with the person whom you're talking to. This is a true sign of self-confidence, don't stare, just look them in the face ...and occasionally smile. If it helps you maintain eye contact, notice during the course of the conversation if it is you or they who avert their eyes first. This little game will make you more conscious of this important part of feeling equal to others.

Whenever possible, choose to sit at the head of the table. Others will perceive you as a confident person and take note of what you say. They will see you as leadership potential and often take your advice.

Walk with a spring in your step. Even if you have nowhere in particular to be, walk quickly as though you have a purpose. Others will perceive you as being self-confident for this.

Speak up and talk clearly. Whether you are in a classroom, workplace, in the butchers or in a seminar, there is nothing worse than trying to hear someone who talks at in inaudible volume. A nice strong voice will show you have self-confidence, make people sit up and take heed of what you're saying, like you more and make you far more likely to secure that job you're being interviewed for. This will gradually increase your self-confidence in public speaking and gets you noticed once again for leadership potential.

Be resolute, not quavering or indecisive.

Be consistent: stick to your ideals and your principles, do not waiver...and be quick to respond.

- **Be a nice person**
Finally, to be a confident person, you need to like yourself. No one will believe in you and like you unless you believe in yourself first. Strive to be everything you admire in others. Be kind to other people; pay them compliments, show them you appreciate them, laugh with them, feel at ease with them, and generally make them want to spend time with you. Maintain your moral standards and stick to your principles. Don't swear in front of children, don't drink to excess, or gamble your money away. There are far more important things in life, and you will be wasting all your hard earned money. You could open a savings account, or even place a jar in the kitchen, where you can drop a few coins whenever you think you have done something admirable or that you feel proud of yourself for. The quantity you invest could be on a scale of, say, one to ten where one unit could be for stopping in the street to give the correct change to someone or holding a door open, on an escalating scale up to a much more worthy achievement of perhaps feeling confident enough to apply for a new job, attend an interview or enter some

type of contest. Note that it is irrelevant whether you actually get the job you have applied for or win that contest you have entered, the point is that you were willing to try and that you felt confident enough to go for it and take on that new challenge. You will then reap the benefits twice over. You may succeed in getting the job or winning a prize for being the best singer in the karaoke but you will also have put away those coins so that later on you can treat yourself to something nice that you have wanted for a long while. That really deserves a pat on the back.

Remember, that whether low self-confidence is circumstantial or chronic, whether it is owing to a result of a lack of faith in your abilities, a perceived lack of attractiveness or relationship skills, there are always ways to improve and provide ourselves with more respect and self-regard. Appreciate yourself for what you are – faults, flaws, foibles, and all. We mustn't go into denial of the problems caused by low self-confidence, to nurture the negative feelings we hold about ourselves, and strengthen them by repeatedly putting ourselves down. Stop berating yourself as it is imperative for our future happiness to deal with these issues right away, and treat ourselves the way we hope that others would. Try and contribute more to the world as a whole and focus less on yourself. No one is perfect – there is no such thing when it comes to the human being. Your abilities and self-image can change over time, acknowledge this, be patient, work at it and adjust. You will see a difference over a period of time.

I hope these hints and tips I have provided you with have helped you to realize what you can now do for yourself, and how you can get more out of life by just listening to some good advice. I wish you lots of luck, but I already have faith in you and next time you feel like you need a pep talk to help you boost your self-confidence, refer to this book for some expert help – it will always be there for you!

If you enjoyed this book or received value from it in any way, then I'd like to ask you for a favor: Would you be kind enough to leave a review for this book on Amazon? It'd be greatly appreciated!

Click the link below to leave a review on Amazon.com
http://www.amazon.com/dp/B00JGWLDKE

SUBSCRIBE TO MY NEWSLETTER

http://eepurl.com/U76qr

Other Books Written by Robert Gallagher

- **Stress Management (An Easy to Understand Book Full of Tips and Tricks to Fight Against Everyday Stress) - http://www.amazon.com/Stress-Management-Understand-Against-Everyday-ebook/dp/B00EAQTKPQ/**

- **Bullying is for Losers (Tips and Tricks on How to Overcome Bullying) - http://www.amazon.com/dp/B00KFII3VU**

- **From Surviving to Thriving (Recovery Guide for Survivors of Abuse) - http://www.amazon.com/dp/B00NG86E1W**

- **Stress Management & Self Confidence (2 in 1) - www.amazon.com/dp/B00Q1M95NY**

Click the link below to leave a review on Amazon.com
http://www.amazon.com/dp/B00JGWLDKE

SUBSCRIBE TO MY NEWSLETTER

http://eepurl.com/U76qr

References

Coleman, J.C. & Hendry, L.B. (1999). The Nature of Adolescence (Third Edition), Routledge, London.

Darley, J. M., Glucksberg S., Kamin, L.J. & Kinchla, R.A. (1984). Psychology. (Second Edition), Prentice-Hall, Inc., New Jersey.

Frydenberg, E. & Lewis, R. (1993). Boys play sport and girls turn to others: gender and ethnicity as determinants of coping. Journal of Adolescence. 16. 253-266.

Leary, M.R. (1999). Making sense of self-esteem. Current directions in Psychology, **8**, 32-35. (pp.43,67).

Rosenzweig, M.R., Breedlove, S.M. & Leiman, A.L. (2002). Biological Psychology. (Third Edition), Sinauer Associates, Inc., Massachusetts.

Noe, P. (2013). The importance of confidence in the workplace. Absolute Confidence. Pp.1.

Myers, D.G. (2002). Social Psychology (7th Edition), The McGraw-Hill Companies, Inc., New York.

Winefield, A., Tiggemann, M., Winefield, H. & Goldney, R. (1993). Growing up with unemployment: a longitudinal study of its impact, Routledge, London.

SUBSCRIBE TO MY NEWSLETTER

http://eepurl.com/U76qr

Made in the USA
Lexington, KY
15 January 2015